WHAT
DAMAGES
RELATIONSHIPS?

WHAT DAMAGES RELATIONSHIPS?

GR8 RELATIONSHIPS

EQUIP PRESS

Colorado Springs

WHAT DAMAGES RELATIONSHIPS?

Published by Equip Press, Colorado Springs, CO

First Edition: 2023
What Damages Relationships? / (GR8 Relationships)
Paperback ISBN: : 978-1-958585-19-1
eBook ISBN: 978-1-958585-20-7

EQUIP PRESS

Colorado Springs

CONTENTS

INTRODUCTION

Relationships become complex because of what we at GR8 Relationships call the *Flashing ME*. Essentially the Flashing *ME* describes a focus on your *ME*, that is, always looking to fulfill what you want and the way you want it, rather than focusing on what is the highest and best for someone else. Worse yet, relationships are further complicated because of the judgments God placed on men and women. We'll look at how this Flashing *ME* and the judgments fuel different behavior for men and women. Since men are designed to work with the role of provider, protector, and preserver and women are designed to relate with the role of helper, nurturer, and supporter, the Flashing ME shows up in different ways.

What is the *Flashing ME*?

When you have problems in a relationship, don't you typically point your finger at the other person? Do you find yourself thinking or saying these phrases?

"You need to do it my way."
"You need to make me happy."
"You need to change." (I am okay, you aren't!)

These phrases are indicators that your ME is flashing. Your ME is flashing? Here's the concept, in case it is new for you.

You might be wondering what *Flashing ME* means. More than likely, it's your biggest problem, and exactly what it sounds like. Your *ME* is your focus. It demands that you serve yourself, demand your way and focus on yourself more than focusing on or serving others.

The fact that you may not see how often you focus on yourself (that is on *ME*) is a sad thought. When other people are selfish and self-absorbed, you notice, but not when you do it. Is that true for you? It is for me.

When others are selfish, it is like they have the word *ME* flashing on their forehead. But when I do it, I cannot see it, because it is on my forehead above my eyes. I can be totally selfish, not interested in serving others, which means my *ME* is flashing brightly enough to light a house, but I do not see it. I can look at this another way and ask myself if I am acting like a baby.

Flashing ME—Different for Men and Women

Since men and women were intentionally designed by God for different roles it makes sense that the

Flashing ME manifests differently in them. Women are designed to *relate*, so they can:

- Naturally and instinctively Help, Nurture and Support.
- Use their relational abilities to serve and meet other's needs.

But when pursuing her own needs, she misuses her design and might try to carefully change her husband to what she wants, and say to herself, "Without him knowing, I will make him the man and husband he should be. I will ultimately be satisfied!"

Or, she might come at it from a different angle by focusing on power to make him change, and think, "I'm going to change him to be the man and husband he should be. I will ultimately be satisfied!"

God designed men with a totally different role in mind, to provide for their families and toil. Men are designed to *work*, so they can:

- Naturally and instinctively – Provide, Protect and Preserve.
- Use their work abilities to serve and meet others' needs.

So, a man's Flashing ME misuses his work and activities design, and he begins to think, "I must be successful so the family can have the things we want (and I can feel significant)."

Another way the Flashing ME plays out for a man is just *get along or give up.* In this case, he is thinking, "I wish I could be significant, so that others would respect me." That thinking results in becoming a "victim," blaming life, circumstances, and people for the direction of his life.

Before we go further, please keep this important thought in mind. Men and women have a design from God and have also developed from interaction with their families, society, and selves. If we act differently than our design, it does not negate the design. Most often, development overlays and prevents us from acting according to our design.

Do any of these scenarios sound familiar to you? Have you seen them in your spouse or yourself? It's likely both of you have an issue with the Flashing ME, and it can and will destroy your relationships if you allow it.

The Flashing ME in Business

Men have a great need for respect in all relationships, whether it's marriage, a governing body of a Church, or business, whereas women have a great need to relate and a desire for others to relate to each other. In the scenario below, make a note of how the *Flashing ME* plays out and how in the scenario, that might impact smooth and efficient business operations.

The scene is an executive retreat in the Rocky Mountains near Aspen, Colorado. The Dynamic Financial Solutions company has been in business for 15 years and has shifted its target market, so they need a re-branding to compete with the competition. The company's core product offerings are business-to-consumer financial products and their target markets are Millennials and younger. Some of the executives in the firm have children who are Millennial-age, so they realize that the younger generation views and manages finances very differently than some of their more established clients. In addition, since they were going to the expense to meet off-site, they decided that each key leader would give a *State of the Business* report for their particular area of expertise.

Most of the executives' spouses are in attendance, as there are several social events planned. The first evening everyone gathers for an informal dinner at the retreat center's main lodge. At this event, some of the executives meet in person and meet spouses for the first time, since the company has corporate offices all over the country. The key players in attendance are described below.

Glenn and Marci Jones

Glenn is the CEO of the firm and co-founded it with Steve Williams, who has since moved to a different company. Marci does not work outside the home. They have three grown children who are 25-30. Glenn and

Marci are in their late-fifties and live in New Jersey, just across the river from Manhattan, where the main corporate offices are located.

John and Maria Gaines

John is the COO of the firm and has worked there since the company's inception. Maria, his wife, is a Learning and Development Consultant with a large company. They have no children, live in Connecticut, and he works in the New York office. They are both in their mid-fifties. Maria was not able to attend the event.

Abraham Jacobson

Abraham is the CIO of the company. He is in his late-twenties, and was recruited from a national consulting firm, where he worked from the time he graduated from MBA school until joining Dynamic Financial Solutions. The firm brought him in a year ago, to help bring a younger perspective to the firm. He is not married and lives by himself in a small apartment in San Jose, CA.

Angela and Trevor Smalley

Angela is the Chief Marketing Officer for the firm and has been with the company for 10 years. Her husband Trevor works in sales for a Food Distributor. They live in Palo Alto, CA and have never met Abraham. They have three children, ages 10-15, and are in their mid-forties. Trevor loves to golf and hiking, so he gladly joined Angela for this event.

Sam and Myra King

Sam is the CFO and lives in Palo Alto California. He was recruited from another Financial Services firm five years ago and did not want to relocate to the East coast. He was born and raised in Georgia, but his kids and grandkids live in California. Myra does not work outside the home. They are in their mid-sixties.

All have a grand time at the informal dinner. The spouses make plans for what they will do the next day while the executives navigate their game plan for re-branding.

Day One

The executives gather in a beautiful conference room with white boards on one wall, lectern and screen at the front, and coffee bar at the back of the room. One wall has floor-to-ceiling windows with a beautiful view of a meadow and the Rockies behind.

Everyone gets quickly situated to get down to business.

Glenn stands at the lectern and makes opening remarks, then turns the meeting over to Angela Smalley for her presentation and initial brainstorming. Angela presents marketing data on their target market that she and her team have gathered in preparation for the meeting. She answers questions from the group, then moves to the whiteboard to facilitate the initial brainstorming.

Sam speaks first, "This is great that we are doing this, because I have been in this industry a while and as you all know it has changed quite a bit as our customer base has aged, and in some cases have transitioned their money to heirs or organizations. I think we need to play on convenience. That's what these young people want. Something that's quick and easy, that they can do from their phone."

Abraham responds, "Everyone says that in their slogans. That's not going to make us stand out."

Angela, noting Sam's look at Abraham's response, reminds everyone that they are brainstorming, so all ideas are welcome at this point. Abraham doesn't respond to this or acknowledge Sam's idea, he just remains silent.

Glenn chimes in and says, "Based on what my children tell me, their biggest concern is quick returns. I think we should play off that some way."

John chuckles and says, "Hey, I just keep the business running. I am not a marketer."

Angela retorts with a smile, "You can't get off that easy. What stood out to you in the data that I presented?"

John said, "Well to Glenn's point, this generation is used to volatile movement in the markets and a *buy-sell-get-out* mode. Many don't have that much money to put anywhere but is that really who we are after anyway. That said, I'm thinking something like, *Quick or Quicker?* as a question to the customer."

Sam didn't say anything, but thought to himself, "Isn't that what I said? They want to do something quick on their phone." He decided just to be quiet, because he was a little annoyed at the situation.

The group continued the discussion and even veered off into new products they might need to develop. Sam warned that whatever they created needed to make financial sense. Abraham responded by saying, "Obviously, I could have told you that."

Sam thought to himself, "Why should I even say anything?"

About that time, the catered lunch arrived in the room. Angela was thinking that she was glad for a break from trying to manage the egos in the room. In her years in business, she always relied on strong relationships with people and doing what she could to maintain relationships among team members. Whether it was executive teams like this one, or her own team, she tried to view things from someone else's perspective.

They enjoyed their lunch, then retired to the golf course for the rest of the afternoon. Sam avoided Abraham, not knowing how Abraham might insult him next. After golf, the spouses joined them for early dinner and conversation on the outdoor patio. Sam and Myra retired early in order to connect with their kids and grandkids on FaceTime.

Day Two

Sam made a conscious decision to keep to himself this morning. He decided the financial aspects of what the team was tackling could be better handled back at the office. No one was going to keep Abraham from insulting him, and he would look like the bad guy if he challenged Abraham or responded to him.

Abraham joined the meeting an hour late. He didn't apologize to anyone or give an explanation. Glenn was presenting, but kept going, since he didn't know why Abraham was late to the meeting and did not want to put him on the spot. But more than that, he was at a key point in the presentation and did not want to lose the audience.

Abraham thought to himself, "These jerks don't even care that I was late to the meeting. What if I had a family emergency or an IT emergency?!"

He slumped in his chair thinking about it. John noticed but decided to ignore it until lunch. He did not want the meeting disrupted. It was obvious that everyone was wondering what was going on with Abraham. They all figured if he didn't let anyone know he would be late or if something was wrong it was because he was young and didn't know how to deal with life very well.

Angela started feeling nervous because she couldn't stand conflict in business meetings. "Can't we just all get along?" she thought. She desperately hoped that Abraham wouldn't *start* something by blurting out something rude or being sarcastic. Then she would have to mend the fence, which would take her focus away from proving to these men that she knew what she was talking about.

John thought to himself with a chuckle, "I am staying out of this drama. This is how I have survived in my career. I just stay out of the way so nobody blames me for what is going on. That's not my job anyway. I just need to focus on keeping the business running. If I get into the politics of the business that will just cause me problems and hurt my chances of survival at this company in the long term."

The morning finished after each leader made a presentation regarding the *State of the Company* in their area of responsibility and answered questions. The group adjourned for the afternoon to enjoy the mountain retreat. No group activities were planned for the afternoon or evening. The next day, all departed early, feeling some level of accomplishment, yet not feeling the cohesiveness of a strong leadership team.

Scenario Questions

1. Describe examples of *Flashing ME* behavior for
    each executive in the story.

Describe examples of *Flashing ME* behavior for each executive in the story.	
CHARACTER	BEHAVIOR

2. What were some of the consequences of these
    behaviors and the underlying *Flashing ME*?

_____

_____

_____

_____

_____

_____

_____

3.　How has this impacted the team overall? How could this impact business performance or working relationships?

_____

_____

_____

_____

_____

_____

_____

_____

4.　What could each person do differently to focus on *serving others best*?

What could each person do differently to focus on *serving others' best?*	
CHARACTER	BEHAVIOR

5. How can you apply this scenario to groups
    you interact with? For example, small group
    meeting with church, non-profit organization
    work, or work relationships you have?

REFLECTIVE QUESTIONS

- What did you notice about the *Flashing ME* that sounds close to your own behavior?

  _____

  _____

  _____

  _____

- How has your own *Flashing ME* impacted your marriage, business or other significant relationships in your life?

  _____

  _____

  _____

  _____

- What do you need to recognize and change about how you interact with others?

  _____

  _____

  _____

  _____

- What exactly can you do to replace your *Flashing ME* with *focusing on their best*?

  _____

  _____

  _____

  _____

  _____

- What will you do when you notice the *Flashing ME* in your spouse or someone else you are in relationship with?

  _____

  _____

  _____

  _____

  _____

- How do you think changing your response to someone else's *Flashing ME* will impact your relationships?

  _____

  _____

  _____

  _____

  _____

UNKNOWN JUDGMENT FOR WOMEN

To the woman He said: "I will greatly
multiply your sorrow and your conception;
In pain you shall bring forth children;
Your desire shall be [a]for your husband,
And he shall rule over you."

Genesis 3:16, NKJV

The above scripture describes what we at GR8 Relationships call the Unknown Judgment for Women. *Unknown* is a good way to describe it based on the fact that so many people are not aware of this judgment. Lack of awareness leads to the notion that some relationships are *just complicated*. People sometimes accept that a relationship *is what it is*, when a deeper understanding of the unknown judgment could help improve the relationship.

Common misconceptions about relationships can be found in day-to-day conversations and in the movies or television programs. Often you will hear someone say, "Our relationship is complicated," or "Our relationship is complex."

Here's a hypothetical conversation you might hear in a movie between two women talking about a relationship.

> *"He has been talking with a woman he used to date and appears to be having second thoughts about me. I can't stand the woman and want her out of our life, but I can't say that, because I'm afraid that it will create more problems with us, and he may choose to go back with her. When I have said something to him, he tells me there is nothing to it, but I don't believe him. So, yesterday he left his phone when he went to the store, and I looked through his texts and emails and found where he has been talking with her. It's so complicated – what can I do?"*

The above is a simple version of movie theme with complicated twists and turns. A number of elements could make the above more complex, and an overlay of beliefs that relationships are complicated only exacerbates the problem.

So what about you? Do you think relationships are complicated? In particular, do you view your own relationships complicated? Most of the time complexity is the result of bad thinking about relationships. They are not as complex when you do them correctly. The complexity comes from doing things wrong.

The fact is that relationships become complex when you make everything about *ME* (yourself) instead of pursuing the other person's best and doing what God asks you to do. Complexity and confusion occur when you are tied up in bad thinking, bad feelings, and bad actions. They are never complex when viewing them from what the Almighty God has asked you to do. That does not mean the relationship is good or healthy because the other person may be Flashing their *ME* and trying to get you to change.

Doing relationships God's way works. Simplifying relationships focuses on you doing what God wants from you. Obeying God is always straightforward and simple; you are either obeying Him or not. When you are not willing to trust that He knows more than you do, you will second-guess Him.

You might even find yourself saying to God, "You want me to forgive him?!? You can't mean that God, after what he has done to me."

Let's get to the core of the *Unknown Judgments about Women*. This will clear up a lot of misconceptions and *bad thinking*, which leads to poor feelings and actions. The context of Genesis 3:6 is a conversation between the serpent and Eve.

> . . . *the woman saw that the tree was good for food, that it was pleasant to the eyes, and a tree*

*desirable to make one wise, she took the fruit and
ate. She also gave to her husband with her, and
he ate.*

Genesis 3:6, NKJV

Immediately after Adam and Eve sinned by doing
the one thing God forbid them to do in the Garden, they
realized they were naked, made clothes out of fig leaves,
and tried to hide from God. When God confronted
them, they tried to blame everyone but themselves,
which only led to judgments, first to the Serpent, then
Eve, then Adam. Here we will only deal with the curses
toward Eve and Adam.

To reiterate, here is the curse toward Eve.

*To the woman He said: "I will greatly multiply
your sorrow and your conception;
In pain you shall bring forth children;
Your desire shall be for your husband,
And he shall rule over you."*

Genesis 3:16, NKJV

This judgment is tough! God designed a woman to
be relational, but this judgment now makes it difficult
to fulfill her relational design.

Ladies, if you experience these problems daily, it
means you are not doing what God asks you to do. By

His grace you have a solution, but if you are not paying attention your sin nature will drive you to live in your judgement.

Three Elements of Woman's Judgment

The three elements are, Pain with Children, Desire for Her Husband, and Ruled by Her Husband. Let's look at each of these more closely

Pain with Children

Pain with children comes with their birth and raising them.

The word *pain* means painful toil. Any woman who has been through labor having a baby can attest to the toil required. Consider Jabez's mother and her childbirth. She says,

> *Now Jabez was more honorable than his brothers,*
> *and his mother called his name Jabez, saying,*
> *Because I bore him in pain.*

1 Chronicles 4:9, NKJV

Childbirth was so painful for her that she named her child after it! As Matthew Henry, author of an exhaustive commentary on the Bible, so aptly describes, a mother's pains of raising children can last for years:

"The sorrows of child-bearing are multiplied;
for they include, not only the travailing throes,
but the indispositions before (it is sorrow from
the conception), and the nursing toils and
vexations after; and after all, if the children prove
wicked and foolish, they are, more than ever,
the heaviness of her that bore them. Thus are the
sorrows multiplied; as one grief is over, another
succeeds in this world."

Matthew Henry[1]

Though the news of this judgment against women is heavy, the good news is that God has a solution. Following His plan for living life and focusing on what you need to do to counteract the natural tendency toward succumbing to the judgment. It goes back to focusing on the highest and best for others.

Desire for Her Husband

Here are the two interpretations of this point that are most prevalent.

1. She so craves a relationship with her husband that she will do anything to have it. Some commentaries interpret this as "a strong sexual and psychological dependence on her husband."

2. She wants to make the relationship go her way. She wants the husband to do whatever she wants him to do.

The first interpretation can be supported by the strong feelings that a woman can have to enjoy a relationship with a man. She is wired to be relational, and it makes sense that she could be consumed with that desire, which could make life miserable when her husband is not responding. In addition, the interpretation is supported when the word for *desire* in Hebrew (*tsuka*) is taken from the Aramaic root for *exciting, loving, or psychological desire.*

Most of the time, men have the stronger desire for sexual fulfillment than women, which does not mean a woman would not want or enjoy sex, but a woman *craving* sex in the relationship is an anomaly. This fact can present difficulty with the first interpretation.

The second interpretation can be more easily supported when the word for *desire* in Hebrew (*tsuka*) is understood as coming from the Aramaic root that means *to compel, to urge, to seek control.*

Additionally, when you look for other occurrences of *tsuka* it shows up in the next chapter of Genesis, when God was talking with Cain about his anger for the Lord not respecting his offering.

If you do well, will you not be accepted? And if you do not do well, sin lies at the door. And its desire is for you, but you should rule over it.

Genesis 4:7, NKJV

Here *desire* is similar to a predator stalking its prey, ready to pounce, the same picture the Lord gives us about Satan.

Whether you agree with the first or second interpretation, you will end up in the same place. When you crave a relationship, or have an unhealthy dependence on it, you will use a stealth strategy to achieve the relationship you need. So, you manipulate others to get your way. You will be wearing a mask, controlling others without being obvious. It will appear that you are doing what they want, but you are trying to get what you want. It doesn't appear controlling although it is.

On the other hand, when you dominate the relationship through aggression, you use force or power as your strategy to create the relationship that meets your needs. You have learned techniques that work for this strategy, especially when the other person does not put up a fight.

Either strategy leads to *control*. Ultimately, the woman living in her judgment does not want to follow or live under the authority of her husband.

This is the consequence of not listening to the Lord and not following what He has shown you to do in His Word.

Though you may not agree with this conclusion, plenty of anecdotal evidence supports it, likely in your own experience. Objectively look at your own behavior over time to see what is true about this conclusion in the way that you act.

Ruled by Her Husband

The last element of a woman's judgment provides additional news on how your husband with relate to you. Look at the part of verse 16.

. . . and he shall rule over you.

Genesis 3:16c, NKJV

Rule is the critical word in this phrase. The Hebrew word is *mashal*, which means to have dominion, reign govern, master, gain control, or have authority. Here are two common interpretations.

The verse is a restatement of man's authority that the Lord has already provided. This is God's order for the family and it is reaffirmed in 1 Corinthians 11:3 that talks about God, Christ, man and woman.

*But I want you to know that the head of every
man is Christ, the head of woman is man,
and the head of Christ is God.*

1 Corinthians 11:3, NKJV

It can indicate harshness, abuse or using the relationship for personal benefit. In Genesis 2, you see that Adam was designated as the authority, to rule.

This is also evident in his judgment from God, "because you have listened to your wife . . ."

And it is evident in the way Adam named Eve as well as the animals. When you name something, you have authority over them.

While authority already belonged to Adam, using that authority and acting harshly toward women would be new now that Adam and Eve had sinned. Before the sin, there was no evidence that Adam was harsh. But, the history of the world reveals a testimony of man's abuse of authority and women.

Both interpretations combined provide reality. Man is the authority at home, as we see in 1 Corinthians 11:3. He is the ruler, even if and when his wife is controlling him. He has this assigned role from God not because he deserves it, because God sees it as the best for order. Since man is selfish, his rule won't always be healthy or appropriate as God intended.

How Judgments Play Out

Let's look at a scenario to demonstrate how the Unknown Judgment for Women (UJW) might look in today's world. As you read the story, look for the three elements of the UJW and how they impact the characters in the story. Also, notice what similarities you see to your own life.

Mary and Rico have been married for 15 years. They are in their early forties and have three children, Joanie is 13, Jason is 11 and Maggie is 4. Mary and Rico both have independent personalities, so marriage required many adjustments. Mary and Rico met on the job in a clothing manufacturing firm, Thrifty Threads, and they both still work for the company. Mary manages four team leaders who supervise workers on the manufacturing line. Rico works in the facilities department and is managed by a remote boss, who meets with him only about once a month. Rico works mostly with contractors, who provide construction or maintenance services to the firm. He does most of his work independent of other teams or people. His boss is pretty hands-off in his management style.

Mary and Rico decide to take a weekend trip alone and leave the kids with Mary's parents, who live about an hour away from them. After they drop the kids off, Mary and Rico start their three-hour drive to their favorite camping site with cabins.

Mary is tired from a tough week at work and with her daughter Joanie, who just turned 13. She started the conversation with a big sigh, "I hope Mom and Dad can handle Joanie. I just don't like the crowd she is hanging around with."

Rico says, "Oh, they will be fine. You worry too much. I mean what kind of trouble could they get into anyway? Your mom watches them like a hawk."

"Rico, your lax attitude is what got her in trouble the last time. You let her go out with those neighbor girls who are up to no good. I know you mean the best for her, but you can't be buddy-buddy with your kids. They will stop respecting you, and I want them to respect you."

"Thanks Mary, I appreciate that."

"Raising Joanie takes so much energy from me. I feel like I'm always second-guessing what she's doing or who she's talking to on the phone, chat, or social media. Who knows what ideas she's getting from Snapchat and TikTok. You know I try to connect with her by taking her shopping or chatting with her in the evenings, but she just tells me she has to study, when I know she doesn't."

"Mary, it sounds like you are offended by her. You want a relationship with her, but she's turning you away."

"Well Rico, you wouldn't know because you don't need to connect with people. You kinda like to connect with things, contracts and processes," she said with a laugh. "13-year-old antics roll off you."

Rico chuckled too, recognizing that Mary was right, to a degree.

"Joanie relates to you better than me, and you are not even that worried about whether you have a relationship with her or not. Maybe you can put in a good word for me?" she laughs.

"Sure, glad to," Rico says, feeling a bit of pride rising up because Mary is asking for his help.

"Rico, I am so tired. When we get to the campsite, can I just read and relax?"

"Sure hon. That's not what I had in mind, but that is fine."

"I appreciate you, Rico. I will make it up to you," she says with a wink.

Rico immediately thinks about how she is going to make it up to him and smiles wryly.

They arrive at the campsite and drive up to their cabin. Mary asks Rico to bring in the bags, she is just too tired to be hauling things inside. She grabs a couple of grocery bags and a small cooler out of the car and goes into the kitchen to check out the amenities. Rico takes all the bags into the bedroom then appears in the kitchen.

"So, what do you want for dinner? I can make your favorite pasta and chicken," she says with a smile, hoping he will choose that dish because it's very easy and quick to make.

"Sure, that will be fine," he agrees. "I'm going to go out and sit on the porch. Come sit with me if you have a break from cooking."

"Oh, you go ahead and relax out there. Can I bring you a glass of tea or water, dear?"

"I'll take a glass of tea."

Rico heads outside to the big Adirondack chairs and plops down to relax after the drive and breathes the country air. He closes his eyes and leans his head back.

Mary comes out with Rico's tea and says, "It will be ready in about 20 minutes, do you want to eat out here? I know how you like the country air."

"Sure. Don't forget to heat the sauce the way I like. What else are you making with that."

"Green beans. You know I always make your favorite dish just the way you like it." She was slightly annoyed at him saying that but didn't show it. She thought to herself, it irritates me when he acts like he's in charge of everything. Like I don't know how to fix his dinner."

When the food is ready, Rico pulls up the small table that's on the porch between the chairs. They eat their dinner making small talk about the kids. Rico asks if she wants to go for a nice walk through the woods, to go watch the sun set.

"You know what, I'm just too worn out from the week. I'm going to take a shower and curl up in bed and read a book."

Rico agrees even though he thinks he can charm her into paying attention to him. He knows just the things to say to get his way with her. "She's an independent woman," he thinks, but she likes for me to be in charge sometimes."

Rico sits on the porch and reads the sports news. Then he looks over financial news, until he finally decides, he's in the country, he should turn off devices. Rico goes inside and finds Mary fast asleep.

"Well now what am I going to do?" he wonders. He saunters to the kitchen to grab a snack even though he isn't hungry. Nothing looks good, so he decides to crawl in bed with Mary.

In the morning, Mary wakes up early and hops out of bed to make Rico his coffee. She brings it into the bedroom along with her tea on a tray. Rico is slowly waking up and sits up in bed to enjoy coffee with her.

Rico says, "So let's hike up the Pine Forest trail today. I miss seeing the view of the lake."

Mary agrees, even though she is not in the mood for a hike. She just wants to keep the peace and not challenge Rico when he has his mind set on something.

As they walk up the trail, Mary talks about her concerns for Joanie. Rico reiterates that she worries too much, and that raising Joanie isn't that bad. At least she's not doing drugs or anything, and she has pretty good grades. He says it's just a phase she is going through and she will grow out of it.

Mary doesn't really agree, but she says, "You're right. She's just a 13-year old growing up. I'll make an effort to stop worrying so much." They continue their hike mostly in silence, just enjoying the gorgeous pine trees along the trail. They stop to eat a snack and take a rest, then go back down the trail toward the cabin.

The next day, they drive back to pick up the kids.

Mary asks her mom, "How did it go?"

"It was perfect," her mom answered. "No problems at all."

Rico caught Mary's eye and raised his eyebrows as if to say, "I told you so."

Mary felt irritated inside but knew it best to let Rico feel he had the upper hand in the situation.

Joanie looked at her parents with a sullen look as she gathered up her belongings and went out to the car. Jason and Maggie were chattering away about all they did and how much fun they had, while Joanie sat silent all the way home.

REFLECTIVE QUESTIONS

- What evidence do you see in this story regarding the first element of the judgment of women, Pain with Children?

  _____

  _____

  _____

  _____

- How do you feel Mary is handling that element according to God's design for her?

  _____

  _____

  _____

  _____

- What evidence do you see of the second judgment element for women, A Desire for Her Husband? How do you think she is handling that according to God's plan?

  _____

  _____

  _____

  _____

- What evidence do you see of the third element, Ruled by Her Husband? What conflicts do you notice are aroused in Mary?

_____

_____

_____

_____

_____

- What dangers do you see in this couple's relationship that need to be addressed?

_____

_____

_____

_____

_____

- What, in this story, do you relate to in your own life?

_____

_____

_____

_____

_____

- What do you need to do to improve your
  relationship with your spouse, or other close
  relationship?

_____

_____

_____

_____

_____

UNKNOWN
JUDGMENT FOR MEN

When you view what God tells you through the window of relationships, it makes His Word even more practical and understandable. The judgments are particularly helpful to me because the effects are so easy to see, but the judgments are not taught in a way to help people see them in relationships and marriages. Unfortunately, they are too often unknown or ignored.

Genesis 3:16-19 will impact every man and woman on the face of the earth until Christ comes again. Each and every relationship struggle has a link back to these judgments. It has proven true in most (probably *all*) of the discussions that my wife, Louie, and I have had with couples struggling in their relationship. I know it is true of my marriage.

Unfortunately, like so much of God's Word, people do not consider it relevant for today, or just no longer in effect. You may refer to Genesis as that "creation story part of the Bible," but the designs and judgments are real. These judgments impact your life right now unless you are walking with the Lord and doing what He asks *real* men and women to do.

So, the man's judgment is described below:

> *Then to Adam He said, "Because you have heeded the voice of your wife, and have eaten from the tree of which I commanded you, saying, 'You shall not eat of it': Cursed is the ground for your sake in toil you shall eat of it all the days of your life. Both thorns and thistles it shall bring forth for you, and you shall eat the herb of the field. In the sweat of your face you shall eat bread till you return to the ground, for out of it you were taken; for dust you are, and to dust you shall return."*

Genesis 3:17, NKJV

What you see in this passage is what Adam did to create his problems and the how his judgment would impact him. First, he listened to someone besides God when deciding what action to take, and therefore sinned. Second, the ground is cursed, which now requires pain and sweat for Adam in order to eat and provide for his family. Third, all his hard work and toil that drives him will only lead back to dust.

Adam's Curse

There are three elements that God states in the judgment issued to Adam. When Eve gave the forbidden fruit to Adam, he followed and did not lead. The second element was not a direct curse to Adam: the ground was cursed, which caused the third element, that Adam's toil would be become painful and he would be returned to dust.

Again, remember the context. Adam and Eve sinned, God issued a judgment on Satan and Eve, now He turns to Adam. God does all things perfectly, right? So, the very order in which He pronounces the judgments is important.

Followed Didn't Lead

When God issued the judgment to Adam starting in verse 17 it is like He is saying this:
"Finally, Adam, you were given the authority to have dominion with Eve over the entire earth. Instead, you abdicated your leadership, listened to, and followed Eve, not Me, and now this entire earth is cursed to be under the dominion of Satan."

Scripture specifically states that Eve was deceived, but Adam was not (1 Timothy 2:14). Unfortunately, many scholars assume this is a good comment about Adam and, therefore, blame Eve for sin, which misses the gravity of Adam's sin.

If you looked at this conversation as a human father talking to his son, it might be, "Adam, you and I had a clear conversation about My expectations for you and Eve. You knew you were not to eat of the Tree of the Knowledge of Good and Evil, but you did it anyway. There are terrible consequences for disobedience and it's going to be painful!"

Like God's judgment upon the woman, the more you understand this judgment, the more aware you will be on how much it affects your life. Then, hopefully you will turn to and choose God's way instead. Since you have read about the woman's judgment, you already have some insight about what God will be doing with the man's judgment.

The first (and probably the most important) lesson for men is the reason God issued the judgment. If you have not let the first part of verse 17 grab your attention, please read it slowly.

> *. . . you have heeded the voice of your wife, and have eaten of the tree of which I commanded you, saying, "you shall not eat of it."*

Genesis 3:17a, NKJV

Here is an especially important question for you, which ties directly to God's statement to Adam. Who is your *Who said so?*

Adam knew the *Who said so,* and chose to replace God with Eve. Are you doing something similar in your life? Is your *Who said so* someone or something other than God?

Your answer to that question lies in what you value and where you spend your time and money. You know the correct answer is God, and probably even say it, but the reality of your time and money shows you the truth. Unfortunately, getting along with others, especially with your wife, can easily become more important than dealing with difficult issues, listening to God, and doing what He says is the right thing to do.

The common sayings, "Happy wife, happy life!" or "If momma isn't happy, nobody is happy!" may be the way a lot of relationships work but that does not make them right. In fact, these sayings likely mean you are not leading, just like Adam did not lead.

The first part of the God's judgment upon the man can easily be distorted, and has been by those with an agenda against women. It is not hard to imagine someone teaching that a husband does not need to listen to his wife because he is the head of the home and makes all decisions. Of course, that is foolishness, easily debunked by the verse itself and by the way that God has called a man to love his wife.

*Husbands, love your wives, just as Christ also
loved the church and gave Himself for her, that
He might sanctify and cleanse her with the
washing of water by the word, that He might
present her to Himself a glorious church, not
having spot or wrinkle or any such thing, but
that she should be holy and without blemish. So
husbands ought to love their own wives as their
own bodies; he who loves his wife loves himself.
For no one ever hated his own flesh, but nourishes
and cherishes it, just as the Lord does the
church. 30 For we are members of His body of
His flesh and of His bones. For this reason a man
shall leave his father and mother and be joined to
his wife, and the two shall become one flesh.*

Ephesians 5:25-31, NKJV

The words most commonly used in the various translations to describe the conversation between Adam and Eve are *listened to*, except for a couple that use *heeded*. In the older translations the words used are *hearkened unto*.

The full impact of the problem is not adequately stated when you only read the words *listened to*, because most people think of it as *hearing* someone. The word *listen* is defined in a variety of ways, as listed below:

- to hear (perceive by ear); to hear of or concerning; to hear (have power to hear);

to hear with attention or interest, listen
to; to hear (of judicial cases)
- to understand (language)
- to grant request
- to listen, give heed, to listen to
- to consent, agree, yield to, to obey, be
obedient

When you consider the gravity of the situation, the last item on the above list: "to consent, agree, yield to, to obey, be obedient." is appropriate. Any of the lesser terms do not convey the gravity of what God was telling Adam.

God is clearly telling Adam, "I am declaring a judgment on you, because you followed Eve, not Me, and that further means you were not leading."

The picture I get in my mind is a private saluting an officer. Adam was saluting Eve and saying, "Yes, ma'am! I'll eat it ma'am!"

Obviously, that picture is a bit over-the-top, but it is much more in line with the context than Adam just listening to what Eve said. The context is about hearing and then doing (or acting on) what Eve told him to do instead of doing what God told him to do.

Adam's judgment was clearly a result of him obeying the wrong person, or the wrong *Who said so*. It has less to do with Adam hearing something and more to do with his will and the decision he made based on what he heard and who said it to him.

Remember the additional context of this passage. This sin in the Garden of Eden happened in the context of a marriage gone wrong. Adam was not protecting Eve and leading her; he was following her, obeying her, and leaving her open and vulnerable. The fact is, you cannot obey and lead the same person at the same time!

Then to add more condemnation on Adam, he was *not* deceived, yet he willingly followed his wife into sin. Let's see what the Apostle Paul says about that.

> *And Adam was not deceived, but the woman being deceived, fell into transgression.*

1 Timothy 2:14, NKJV

He was much more the sinner in this situation than Eve because he was not deceived; at least Eve had that as an excuse. Adam had heard the command directly from God because Eve had not been created when that command was given by God. He knew the command and had no valid excuse, because he was not even deceived by the serpent. He acted based on what Eve said, the one he was supposed to protect and provide for.

The Ground is Cursed

The second element of the judgment is that the ground is cursed. If you stop there, that may not sound that bad for Adam, but God follows with four new things that will now be part of Adam's (and your) existence.

One: Toil will be required in order to eat.

Two: Thorns and thistles will grow from the ground.

Three: Herbs of the field will be a food source.

Four: Sweat will be required to eat bread.

Though the second curse was not directly placed on Adam, it would cause him pain throughout his life. God created this amazing, perfect environment of the Garden of Eden and the entire earth. Now, the very thing that God told Adam and Eve to take dominion over (recounted in Genesis 1:28) rebels against them.

You may have noticed a difference in the woman's and man's judgments. The woman was judged directly. Her very nature and being was judged. With the man, his nature and being were indirectly judged through the curse that God placed on the ground.

What does it mean that the ground is cursed? The ground will no longer participate with Adam in accomplishing the work to be done. Before the judgment, Adam did not need fertilizer. The seed that was planted would grow, and no matter what Adam did the growth of the seed would continue to go in the right direction. No weeds grew. The ground partnered perfectly with him. But after the curse, the ground became hostile to his efforts and work! Adam would now have pain in his work. The earth that Adam worked became hostile and would no longer easily respond. The lack of response from the ground created *toil* for Adam. That word toil in the Hebrew only occurs three times in the Bible, and it occurs first in Genesis 3:16. It is the same word used for the *pain* that a woman will have in childbirth.

A woman experiences pain in her relationships. A man feels pain in his work. Our perfect God creates the perfect judgments. Both man and woman have pain, and that pain is directly linked to the judgments God placed on them respectively.

Men deal with this pain differently. Some men give up, because of the pain and become irresponsible. Others work harder trying to beat the pain and become workaholics. But none ever control their work. The weeds always grow back; what was done becomes undone again.

From Dust to Dust

Finally, the ground will take him back as dust. The earth was what Adam was created from and he will now die and turn back to dust.

Men, this judgment attacks you at your core. God designed you with a need to be significant, but the judgment works directly against that need. Its effect reinforces the reality that you were made from dust and you will return to it. All the work you do will eventually need to be redone.

The law of entropy prevails. Entropy is a measure of the disorder or randomness in a closed system. The inevitable and steady deterioration of a system or society. Both judgments reinforce entropy – a disorder in relationships for women and in work for men, which is the way sin works in and on all of us and God's creation.

Just like the woman's judgment, God did not leave you without a way out. He has a solution. Every invitation and instruction He has given to men about how He wants you to think, act, and feel is part of His solution to your judgment. Obviously, the solution starts with the inner working of the life of Christ, but it requires a choice to live for righteousness, not unrighteousness.

The Judgment is *reality*. You and I may not like it, but this is the way that it is, not just how it feels. Not wanting it to be this way is a typical method of trying to remove the pain, but it does not work. It is this way, and it does not feel good. Whether you agree or not does not make it untrue. People can tell you about your lack of leadership in the home, unhealthy focus on establishing your identity based on your work and activities, but you are the one who needs to do something about it. Are you willing to see this as reality or deny it?

Your judgment as a man will focus your attention on work and activities, but the ground will not cooperate, and it will take pain and sweat to produce results. Without doing life God's way, work will be painful and unfulfilling.

That difficulty at work will combine with the judgment on women to create further relationship problems. The more difficult the relationships, the more you may focus on work in order to be significant there, because you are not feeling or just are not significant at home.

You can unlock the solution by accepting the way that God has designed men. God's description of a real man is in Titus 2, which includes the solution for all relationships.

Work and Providing

Please note that work is not the curse, it just leads back to dust; work is no longer fulfilling as it was before the fall. To get the full impact of this judgment, do you remember how Adam – and all men – are designed? Go back to chapter 2 in Genesis:

> *before any plant of the field was in the earth and*
> *before any herb of the field had grown. For the*
> *Lord God had not caused it to rain on the earth,*
> *and there was no man to till the ground*

Genesis 2:5, NKJV

Then the Lord God took the man and put him in the garden of Eden to tend and keep it.

Genesis 2:15, NKJV

Why is looking at our design so important? Man's judgment directly impacts his design! Just like the woman's relational design is impacted by her judgment, the same linkage is true for man and his design and judgment.

REFLECTIVE QUESTIONS

For Men

- Think of the first part of Adam's judgment, that he followed what Eve said instead of following what God told him about the fruit on the Tree of Knowledge. How do you see this playing out in your own life? Are you trying to please your wife to keep peace, or please God? Describe your situation below.

_____

_____

_____

_____

- Think of the second part of the judgment, that the ground is cursed. How is that impacting your life right now?

_____

_____

_____

_____

_____

- Based on the third part of the judgment (that man came from dust and will be returned to dust) how does that impact your attitude toward your work? How does that impact your feeling of significance? What does this third part imply for your relationship with others, and especially God?

_____

_____

_____

_____

_____

For Women

- Based on man's judgment that he followed what Eve said, instead of what God commanded, what if anything can you change in the way that you relate to your husband or betrothed?

_____

_____

_____

_____

_____

- How can you support your husband or
  betrothed in his work? With you, relationships
  need to be maintained and mended. With him,
  work needs to be maintained and mended.
  How can you be a support for him?

  _____

  _____

  _____

  _____

  _____

- Stand in your husband or betrothed's shoes,
  how do you notice the concept of dust to dust
  impacting him? This part and the painful toil
  directly impact a man's desire for significance.
  How can you help, not nag, him to pursue
  significance at home instead of primarily
  through work and activities?

  _____

  _____

  _____

  _____

  _____

THE BATTLE BETWEEN DESIGN AND JUDGMENTS

This graphic depicts the best structure for life. You will experience the least resistance in the path when you focus on the end result—or the *There*—of glorifying God. No matter what your *Here* (or current reality) is, when you focus on ultimately glorifying God, you will likely live within your design, love others, and trust and depend on God.

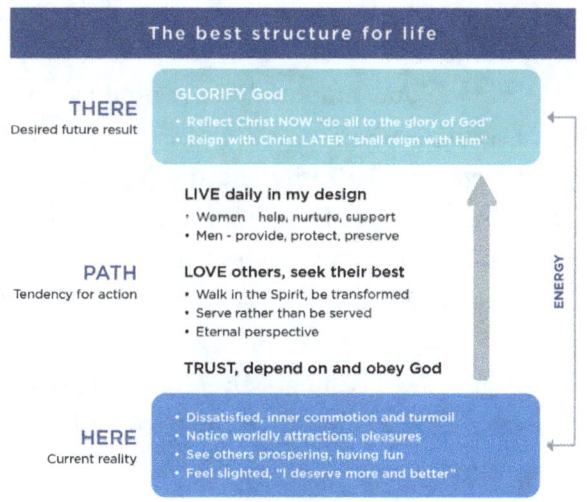

The best structure for life

THERE
Desired future result

GLORIFY God
• Reflect Christ NOW "do all to the glory of God"
• Reign with Christ LATER "shall reign with Him"

LIVE daily in my design
• Women - help, nurture, support
• Men - provide, protect, preserve

PATH
Tendency for action

LOVE others, seek their best
• Walk in the Spirit, be transformed
• Serve rather than be served
• Eternal perspective

TRUST, depend on and obey God

HERE
Current reality

• Dissatisfied, inner commotion and turmoil
• Notice worldly attractions, pleasures
• See others prospering, having fun
• Feel slighted, "I deserve more and better"

ENERGY

Unfortunately, the judgments against men and women cause you to misuse your design. The curses are directed at who you as a man or woman were designed to be. As a man, you want to feel significant, so you go off to work. As a woman, you want people to relate to you in the way that suits you, which encourages you to try to control relationships.

The underlying issue with the battle between design and judgment is people focusing on themselves rather than glorifying God. At GR8 Relationships we refer to that as the Flashing *ME*.

The Real Issue—The Flashing Me

As stated before, your *Flashing ME* is your biggest problem. It is what it sounds like. Your *ME* is your focus. It demands that you serve yourself, demand your way and focus on yourself more than focusing on or serving others.

Why do you suppose I am reminding you about your Flashing ME?

I have found I easily and quickly justify making everything about ME and not see my selfish, self-absorbed thinking and actions. That is a sad thought. But when other people are selfish and self-absorbed, I notice.

While the Flashing ME is good to remember, seeing myself as a baby is even more powerful.

Start asking yourself if you are acting like a baby. A baby needs someone to do everything for them. The baby cries until someone meets his needs. That is a sick picture of an adult!

Alternative Structure

The structure in the graphic above is not the only operating structure available to you. Choice is common to all men and women. While you may have little or no choice with things external, you have complete choice on the thoughts and intents of your mind. Unfortunately, this reality is often unrealized or ignored, which results in major problems for people, especially in their relationships.

The reality of where you are now, which is the *Here*, is the result of past choices, but is your current reality. That reality is not based on your perception. You may like or dislike current reality, which includes your current circumstances, relationships, and life; nonetheless, it is the *reality* of where you are right now.

Your current circumstances may be largely, if not totally, out of your control. That does not mean you are stuck. You are always free to choose. The more you believe you are stuck, the less chance you will see choices and options for a different path for your life.

Since choice is available to all mankind, the fundamental choice of life is: will I trust God, or will I trust something or someone other than God? The path of least resistance you take is completely dependent upon where you are (*Here*) and where you want to be (*There*). Obviously, the *There* for the designs and the judgments are different, so the paths are different, too.

This is an easy choice, but it will not appear easy. The only way you will choose the best path, which is the path of your design, is to deliberately make that choice. Following the path of the Judgment can and does happen by deliberate choice, but most often it is followed by not choosing to follow God's way. That choice is more like auto-pilot in an airplane.

You will live in judgment unless you renew your mind to follow God and His ways. Simply reacting and responding to life puts you in the path of the judgment. Always be thankful for your current circumstance and place God (and God's Word) first in your mind. Otherwise, you will follow your sin nature and the path of the judgments.

Your mind must constantly be renewed and bathed in truth. Walking with God in the energy of His Spirit will remind you that you belong to God. He will energize your new life and turn off the auto-pilot of your depravity when you choose to live the reality of your new life in Christ. God's reality for us can be difficult to understand.

The *reality*: I am a child of God, freed from slavery to sin.

The *reality*: I do have a sin nature, and the free choice to sin all I want.

Both are real.

But do not forget this *additional* reality. God tells you that the reality of your sin nature has been overridden by the reality of the life of Christ in you. Christ dwelling in you has already occurred and is present daily, whether it manifests in and through your actions or not.

Instead of working through those wonderful and eternal truths, let's focus on how those two real elements show up in the Judgment and Design structures for women and men.

Women—Judgment Versus Design

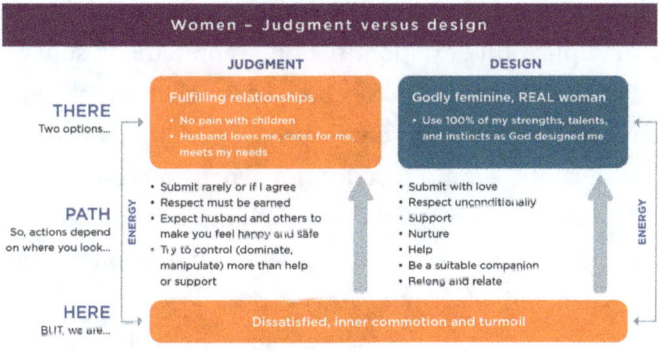

You were born with a design that is fulfilled primarily through relationships. The Judgment focuses your attention on having fulfilling relationships without a focus on the primary relationship with God. It further encourages independence rather than dependence.

Walking in the Spirit, which enables you to live in your design, operating as God desires, is the only way to actually fulfill that design, but the judgment encourages you to believe and act differently. Remember the woman's judgment in Genesis 3:16? You focus on trying to get your husband and children to relate to you to meet your relational needs. While not specifically stated in the woman's judgment, my speculation is this also applies to all of a woman's relationships, married or not. Trying to get those relationships to meet your needs, as opposed to God doing that, means you are living in your judgment.

If that is your focus, the path of least resistance creates actions like trying to control through manipulation or domination more than support. Perhaps you expect your husband or others to make you feel happy and safe, respect people conditionally if they earn it, and submit to a decision when you agree with it. If you see yourself with that thinking, you are following the Judgment structure, focused on the wrong results. Remember, *where you look, you tend to go.*

But if you choose to focus on being a godly woman, your actions are based solely on what God asks of you, not on how to get something from others. You belong and relate to others because that is how you are designed. You begin to understand that fulfilling relationships start with your desire to help, nurture and support those around you. You choose to respect and submit because God invites you to do so. Not because you have to do it.

Men—Judgment Versus Design

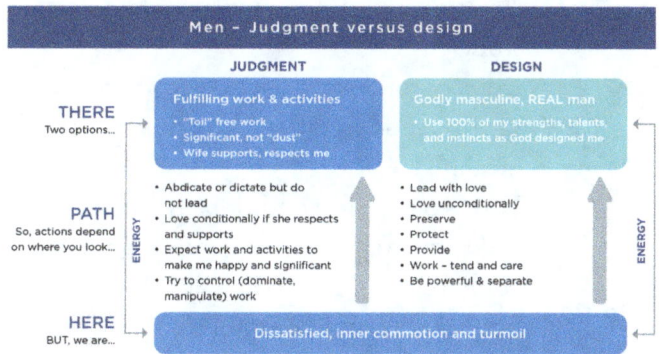

Your situation is similar to women in terms of the structures but quite different in the actions and the way you will be fulfilled or struggle. You were born with a design to be fulfilled, even significant, through your work and activities.

Now with the judgment, that work can be fulfilling, but the fulfillment is fleeting and exacts a toll from you because it is no longer pain-free or toil-free. You will work hard to attain some semblance of significance, which is also fleeting. And you definitely want your wife to see you as significant, especially regarding her respect for you. You want your wife to see you as significant and the temptation will be to seek your own glory through work. What is the intent of your heart? To glorify God or yourself? Ask yourself whether you want to glorify God or yourself.

When you focus on *ME* the path of least resistance creates actions like those listed below:

- Try to control (manipulate, dominate) work.
- Expect work and activities to make you happy and significant, and give you meaning.
- Love your wife conditionally when she is demonstrating respect and support for you.
- Abdicate your leadership or become a dictator, both of which are self-serving and not true leadership.

Again, those are just representative statements, but there is a probable correlation to your life. And what does that imply? *Where you look, you tend to go!* You are focused on the wrong end result.

But if you choose to focus on simply being a Godly man, your actions are based solely on what God has asked of you, not on how to get something from work or others. You demonstrate actions like what is listed below.

- Being powerful and separate in order to benefit others, not yourself.
- Work to provide, protect, and preserve those around you.
- Love unconditionally, even when your wife or others show no respect to you.
- Lead with the intent of pursuing the best for others, even sacrificing for them.

When you focus on being a Godly man, a real man, you fulfill the very essence of how God has designed you. You begin to understand that a fulfilling life involves providing, protecting, and preserving those around you, even when they are not doing anything in return. You choose to love unconditionally, because God has invited you to that godly behavior, not because someone deserves it or because you have to.

You lead not for the glory of being a leader, but because it demonstrates your love and that you want the best for those around you. This is a completely different life that is led by the Spirit rather than your flesh, a life that pursues the glory of God and not the glory of self.

REFLECTIVE QUESTIONS

- Reflect on moving from *Here* to *There*. What is your current reality – your *Here*? What is your focus in life? Are you trying to glorify God? Be objective, not subjective: how it is, not how it feels.

_____

_____

_____

_____

_____

_____

- If you are not focused on glorifying God, what specifically is getting in your way? List some attitudes or activities you could change to move your focus to glorifying God.

_____

_____

_____

_____

_____

_____

- How is God's Judgment versus Design impacting your life personally? What impact is it having on relationships? Positive or negative?

_____

_____

_____

_____

- Describe some recent situations when you operated according to your design because you felt you *had* to.

_____

_____

_____

_____

- Describe some situations when you operated out of your design because you felt joy and fulfillment doing it.

_____

_____

_____

_____

_____

_____

- What do you want to do to start operating freely, according to your design, so life is more fulfilling and joyful?

_____

_____

_____

_____

Daily Tracker

At the end of your day, take a few minutes and look at your day as a video. Look specifically for times you were flashing your ME, making life about yourself. How could you have served someone (lived in your design) rather than yourself (your judgment) in those times? This will help you learn to walk in the Spirit instead of the flesh (Galatians 5:19-22).

DATE	ACTIONS BASED ON DESIGN	ACTIONS BASED ON JUDGMENT

BATTLE BETWEEN DESIGNS AND JUDGMENTS

O bviously, a battle exists between the design and judgment. This battle is an oscillation between two structures, literally between good and evil! The wonderful way that God designed women and men is still true and part of us, but it may not be the primary structure driving our behavior.

When Adam and Eve chose to disobey God, sin entered the world and introduced some big changes. Some of the big changes for them and ultimately for us, compared to their previous life before the sin are listed below:

- Disobedient: no longer primarily obedient to God and honoring Him.
- Guilty: no longer innocent. Obviously, they tried to hide their guilt as evidenced by their actions to cover their nakedness and shift the guilt to others, including God.

- Separated: no longer connected to God, walking with Him in the Garden.
- Exposed: no longer protected and in a safe place. No longer did they have abundant provision, they had to take care of themselves. The structure changed to getting rather than giving and serving.
- Irresponsible: no longer trustworthy. They gave more attention to comparing themselves to others, deflecting responsibility, and blaming others. Instead of focused attention on being trustworthy they exerted more energy regarding how others could not be trusted.
- Fearful: no longer free of cares and concerns. This is probably the biggest change, because fear was a common emotion driven by all of the changes. Each of the changes and judgments demand fear because sin creates separation from the *perfect* Protector, Almighty God. It is easy to see, even in our most honest times, how much protection we need!

Fear is injected into anything you might be thinking about, including everything listed below:

- fear of needs not being met
- fear of losing control

- fear of failing
- fear of not measuring up
- fear of loneliness
- fear of pain
- fear of submitting
- fear of not knowing
- fear of serving others

The judgments also increase the fear that our design needs will not be met. Those fears and many others are fueled by the judgments because sin changed Adam and Eve from a primary focus on God to *ME*.

The judgment structure demands behavior to fulfill your God-given designs by focusing on *ME*. But the design structure demands behavior to fulfill your design by focusing on God and what He wants. These two structures operate simultaneously creating an oscillation between judgment and design.

Women's Battle

Let's look deeper into the battle women experience. As you have seen, the judgment creates a separate structure that is different from the design structure. But keep this in mind, the judgment uses the needs of the design to focus energy on self or *ME* rather than using the design for its created purpose.

That means her judgment encourages and even produces fear that her relational needs will not be met.

That fear removes the focus from serving others to serving self or self-absorption and in turn a desire to control relationships so she can get her needs met.

When a woman is not, or does not feel, safe and protected that is her design speaking, and a function of sin and the judgments. That basic need encourages manipulation and domination as a means to meet her relational needs and to feel safe. Thoughts like:

- "My husband *must* make me *feel* safe, loved, and cherished. He must act according to my needs."
- "My children *must* create no problems. They must be 'pain free.'"
- "I *must* take care of myself, be independent, and not depend on him, because he isn't relating to me as I want."
- "I must *have security in my job, life, relationships*—no matter the cost!"

You may not identify with the statements above because you say them differently. For example, you may say that your husband isn't making you feel safe, your children are creating problems, and you can't depend on anyone but yourself. Whatever your way to say it is the judgment speaking.

The judgment encourages self-dependence and self-absorption, which makes life about *ME* and making things worse, because women are designed to be protected, not be the protector. Her focus is on others as the problem, instead of focusing on what God desires of her.

This does not mean that every relationship she has operates this way, but it will impact her relationship with her husband and children. What about a woman who does not care about her relationship? What if she wants to get away from her husband or even her children? Is she outside the impact of her judgment? No, she still experiences the judgment. Now she experiences the consequences of the judgment, which has brought her to the point of wanting to get away from her husband and children. She is still trying to control relationships or remove pain, but now she is giving up on them. This is like her saying, "I'll show you! I quit!" She wants relationships her way, and if she cannot have them her way, she will not have them at all. The judgment still affects her, and she will experience great pain, because she is walking away from what she was designed for in the first place. Dependence on God is the solution!

The judgment deceives you into thinking you can fulfill your design on your own. You will try to relate based on your own thinking, which will result in being manipulative or dominant, and that in turn leads to frustration, driving your husband, children, and other people away from you. And, when you get to a certain point, you may just give up on the relationships, but the judgment is still at work.

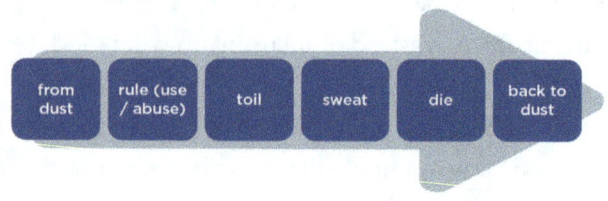

Without dependence on God, your life as a woman becomes like Genesis 3:16. You come from dust, and after child-pain, husband-pain, and being ruled, you will die and return to dust. With that uplifting statement, you are really encouraged and ready for the day, right? (NOT.)

Where is the encouragement? Where is the opportunity for resolution? Where is the way out? The solution is dependence on God and what He invites you to be as a *real* woman. As a *real* woman you want to live with God's Word as your guide and foundation. God designed you to fulfill the qualities, values, and actions that He desires of godly women. God perfectly designed you to fit your role and everything He asks you to do. Look at the passage from Genesis:

> *And the Lord God said, "It is not good that man should be alone; I will make him a helper comparable to him."*
>
> **Genesis 2:18, NKJV**

Helper and Comparable (or suitable) are two critical elements of your design. Though it may not seem so based on the world's view, *helper* is an elevated role. It does not mean you are less than a man. Primarily, you are a helper of God. God wants you to be a helper, just like He is our helper. He wants you to be a **T**ender, **O**pen-hearted **U**ltimate **G**odlike **H**elper, which stands for TOUGH. You can be TOUGH in God's way and maintain your femininity.

Scenario for the Women's Battle

Though the battle between Design and Judgment obviously damages relationships between husband and wife, it plays out in other situations as well. Let's look at a situation in a family.

Maven has four grown daughters who range in age from 37-45. All of them live different states, apart from Maven. The girls' father, Andrew, died in an accident 15 years ago, and Maven has since remarried Allen. Allen had a debilitating stroke a year ago and is unable to work or take care of Maven financially. Maven's husband's condition has left her feeling isolated and *out of control.* She longs for someone to give her a sense of security that she felt with both Andrew and Allen.

She doesn't want to be a burden to her daughters, but she finds herself saying things to her girls that indicate her need for attention, without directly saying it. All the girls feel terribly guilty about their mother's situation, but they all have their own families to care for. Here's a conversation between Maven and her youngest daughter, Amber, who is married with three kids ages 6, 5 and 2.

"How are you doing Mom?' Amber asks during their weekly phone call.

"Oh . . . I'll be okay. I'm just overwhelmed today."

"I know that is so hard for you." Amber said.

"I just wish you and your sisters did not live so far away."

"Gosh, I know that's hard on you Mom," Amber replied. She was careful not to offer help that she wasn't really able to provide. Amber knew there was no way they could move closer to her mom, but her mom did not want to move to where Amber and her family lived.

"I just can't leave here. It's where my friends and church are."

"That's tough Mom. Aren't there friends from church who can help you out?"

Suddenly, Maven got irritated and said, "People from church are not the same as family. You just don't understand! I need the comfort of family around! My parents were married for 60 years and never had to face this feeling of insecurity."

Amber tried to console her mom as best she could but wasn't sure where to go with the conversation next. Countless times she invited her mother to move closer to where she and her family lived so they could help her out, but her mother refused to move from where she lived.

Scenario Questions

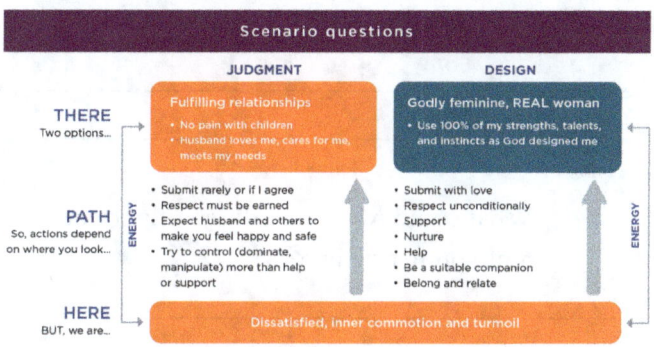

1. Based on the chart above, what do you see going on with Judgment versus Design with Maven?

    _____

    _____

    _____

2. Identify statements Maven makes or behaviors she displays that are manipulative. Based on what you learned about Judgment versus Design for Women, why is she acting manipulative?

    _____

    _____

    _____

3. How is Maven's struggle with Judgment versus Design impacting her family relationships?

_____

_____

_____

4. What could Maven do differently to focus more on her design?

_____

_____

_____

Men's Battle

A man's judgment operates in the same pattern, but creates different fears. His judgment encourages and even produces fear that even his best work will not make him significant. His judgment will produce the fear that even if the work is significant, it still is not enough. He will be left with thoughts like the following:

- "My work and activities *must* make me *feel* significant and respected."
- "My wife *must* make me *feel* significant and respected."
- "My work, activities and wife must be controlled so that it is not painful to me."

As I said to the women, you may not identify with the statements above because you have different ways to say it. For example, you may talk about your recent hunting or business success, how your wife does not appreciate what you provide for her, and you wish you could have some peace at home and more satisfaction with your life and job. Whatever your way to say it, is the judgment speaking.

Again, the judgment demands self-dependence and self-absorption, "Make life about ME," which causes men to focus on others as the problem, instead of what God desires him to focus on.

This leaves a man with a sense of striving, yet not achieving enough. He focuses on getting his design to meet his needs rather than the needs of others. That is what makes the judgments for men and women so powerful. They fuel a self-absorbed mind!

But what if a man does not want to work, accomplish, and be significant? What if he is laying on the couch, drinking beer and doing nothing productive all day? Is he outside the impact of his judgment? Again, no. He, too, is experiencing the consequences of his judgment that brought him to the point of being a couch potato. He still tries to control work by proving he doesn't need it: "You can't control me. I will show you! I quit!" The judgment still impacts him. His efforts to ignore work and significance are just as futile as trying to master work. Neither will bring the significance he wants.

It would be interesting to see what research shows about men who are not working. My speculation is they strive in some way to be significant. For example, one of the stereotypes for some younger men depicts them living at home in their parents' basement playing video games. My guess is they seek significance through the games. The solution, however, can only be found in dependence on God.

The judgment deceives you into thinking you can fulfill your design on your own, causing you to seek significance and control in your work. You will be consumed with work and activities with less or no attention to other things. Instead of fulfillment this leads to pain and frustration because the significance hole can never be filled. The graphic below shows the ugly progression.

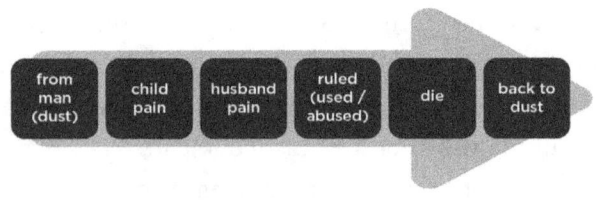

Men, without dependence on God, your life becomes like Genesis 3:17-19.

> . . . *"Cursed is the ground for your sake;*
> *In toil you shall eat of it*

All the days of your life.
Both thorns and thistles it shall bring forth for you,
And you shall eat the herb of the field.
In the sweat of your face you shall eat bread
Till you return to the ground,
For out of it you were taken;
For dust you are,
And to dust you shall return."

Genesis 3:17-19, NKJV

While both women and men suffer physical death eventually, nothing in the woman's judgment specifically speaks of death, as it does in the man's judgment. That could be attributed to man's design being work related. He desires an outcome, impact, accomplishment, and significance. Instead, he will toil and sweat and turn back to dust.

Woman's judgment may not need to talk about death and dust, because she simply wants to relate and feel secure in relationships. Pain in her relationships is the ultimate pain for her. Being and relating is not looking at significance, just belonging. Also, death does not appear to cease relating to others. Scripture implies that relationships have lasting impact. Marriage relationships are different than other types of relationships.

Judgment does not produce uplifting thoughts for men. The solution is dependence on God and what He invites a *real* man to be. Real men demonstrate godliness, so obviously they are more focused on glorifying God than themselves or meeting their self-centered needs.

Scenario for the Men's Battle

Given Men's design to Provide, Protect and Preserve and the three elements of his judgment (following and not leading, the ground being cursed, and return to dust as a result of his toil), let's look at a work scenario and how it impacts a husband-wife relationship.

Jerrod works for a local construction company framing homes and performing finish-out woodwork. His wife Mary is expecting their first child in two months. At the end of the day on a Friday Jerrod's boss informs him that due to a downturn in the Real Estate market, he can only afford to pay one framer/woodworker, so that Jerrod's job will be ending in two weeks.

Jerrod feels total panic even though he doesn't show it on the outside. The tightness in his chest makes him wonder if he is having a panic or worse, a heart attack. He is full of fear about what his wife will say, what she will think about the situation, and how she will act. He cannot help but wonder why the boss let him go and not the other guy. Jerrod arrives earlier to work each day and feels he does superior work compared to the other guy. He thinks about how the boss just doesn't respect him and the work he produces. He works himself into a personal fit of silent anger.

When he arrives home, he explains the situation to his wife, who is not at all understanding. She accuses him of not being prepared to be a father and not working in a steady industry, which has put them in this mess. He retorts by telling her that she can't seem to control how much money she spends on frivolous items. They continue to argue until he says he's had enough for today and that he has to "go out" for a while. He leaves the house, climbs into his truck, and drives aimlessly, thinking through the events of the day. He isn't really even headed anywhere, just trying to figure out how to escape his mess.

Scenario Questions

1. How do you see Jerrod's fears at play based on Judgment versus Design?

_____

_____

_____

2. What would have been a better course of action for him instead of driving off in his truck?

_____

_____

_____

3. How could this scenario impact his
    relationship with his wife? How could it
    impact his relationship with God?

_____

_____

_____

_____

Your Focus

Your focus dictates whether you live in the
problem and your Judgment or in the *solution* and your
Design. Where you look determines the kind of man
you will be because *structure demands behavior. Real*
men focus and depend on God. That removes cultural
confusion, distorted definitions, and the power of
Problem and Judgment structures. Ultimately *real*
men **W**alk **I**n **M**ercy and **P**ower **S**elflessly, which
creates the acronym WIMPS. The building blocks for
men and women walking in the right way are found
in Titus 2.

> . . . *speak the things which are proper for sound
> doctrine*
>
> **Titus 2:1, NKJV**

What does the term *sound doctrine* bring to mind?

Consider what Paul says about doctrine. It protects the reputation of God's Word.

> *. . . that the word of God may not be blasphemed.*

Titus 2:5, NKJV

> *. . . in doctrine showing integrity, reverence, incorruptibility . . .*

Titus 2:7, NKJV

God tells real men something extremely important; sound doctrine is about how you live! The truism *actions denote character* is what God is telling you. *Real* men and *real* women do not just know what the Lord asks them to do, they do it! Actions will eventually show who you really are on the inside. What you know becomes what you show.

Everything Paul talks about here is not specifically about knowledge, but it is about teaching God's word with the end result being men and women who choose to live their lives according to what God asks.

REFLECTIVE QUESTIONS

1. Some of the biggest changes in the lives for Adam and Eve after they entered into sin are listed below. How do you see these playing into your own life?

- Disobedient: no longer primarily obedient to God and honoring Him.

_____

_____

_____

_____

_____

_____

- Guilty: no longer innocent. Obviously, they tried to hide their guilt as evidenced by their actions to cover their nakedness and shift the guilt to others, including God.

_____

_____

_____

_____

_____

_____

- Separated: no longer connected to God, walking with Him in the Garden.

_____

_____

_____

_____

- Exposed: no longer protected and in a safe place. No longer did they have abundant provision, they had to take care of themselves. The structure changed to getting rather than giving and serving.

_____

_____

_____

_____

- Irresponsible: no longer trustworthy. They gave more attention to comparing themselves to others, deflecting responsibility, and blaming others. Instead of focused attention on being trustworthy more energy was exerted regarding how others could not be trusted.

_____

_____

_____

_____

- Fearful: no longer free of cares and concerns. This is probably the biggest change, because fear was a common emotion driven by all of the changes. Each of the changes and judgments demand fear because sin creates separation from the *perfect* Protector, Almighty God. It is easy to see, even in our most honest times, how much protection we need!

_____

_____

_____

2. How does fear impact you? These are ways that are listed in this chapter. Which one resonate with you. What impact do these fears have on relationships?
- fear of needs not being met

_____

_____

- fear of losing control

_____

_____

- fear of failing

_____

_____

- fear of not measuring up

_____

_____

- fear of loneliness

_____

_____

- fear of pain

_____

_____

- fear of submitting

_____

_____

- fear of not knowing

_____

_____

- fear of serving others

_____

_____

- Think about a time when you tried to fulfill your design instead of depending on God. Describe it below. What were the results of doing that?

_____

_____

_____

_____

- Reflect on being a *real* man or woman based on the content in this chapter. How well do you represent God's plan for a real man or woman? What do you need to change? What do you need to keep the same?

_____

_____

_____

_____

- For women: have you heard yourself saying or thinking these things?
  - "My husband *must* make me *feel* safe, loved, and cherished, and act according to my needs."
  - "My children *must* create no problems, and help me be 'pain free.'"
  - "I *must* take care of myself, be independent,

and not depend on him, because he isn't relating to me as I want."

If so, how have these thoughts impacted your attitude toward your children or husband? What event or situation in your life has caused you to make these statements? How can you deal with that event in your life to heal or improve it?

_____

_____

_____

_____

_____

_____

_____

_____

- For men: have you heard yourself thinking or saying these things?
    - "My work and activities *must* make me *feel* significant and respected."
    - "My wife *must* make me *feel* significant and respected."
    - "My work, activities and wife must be controlled so that it is not painful to me." What is the root cause of your attitude, either positive or negative. Think about

your relationship with your earthly
father. How did he impact your attitude
toward family and your spouse. How can
you impact your sons and daughters in a
positive way?

_____

_____

_____

_____

_____

_____

_____

_____

JUDGMENTS AND MARRIAGE

Judgments Help Marriages Fail

Understanding the real problems that the judgments create for men and women simplifies understanding the problems in relationships and marriages that seemed so complex before.

When you grasp the underlying foundation of the image of God, designs and judgments, relationships between men and women will stop looking like some of Albert Einstein's abstract math equations. And, understanding the links between the judgments, designs, and self-absorption (or the Flashing *ME)* you gain new insight into your behavior and those things that help and hurt marriages.

For example, the graphic below represents what the judgments do to marriages. It is simple enough that you can look at it and have some basic understanding of what it is saying without knowing about designs and judgments. However, if you understand the foundation of the chart, it becomes a tool to help a couple through a difficult time.

Most people could look at the chart and have a *that makes sense* or *yeah, I have seen that,* reaction, but would consider it only one of hundreds of things that can happen. Knowing what you currently know from God's Word regarding a man and woman's design and their judgments, you can see that the chart represents a *root cause* for marriage problems and failure.

When you add to the chart the typical comments men and women make, it demonstrates the pain they are feeling in the relationship. A woman might say something like the following:

- "You spend so much time at work and so little time with me and the kids."
- "Your golf is more important to you than your family."
- "Why can't we have some time for just us?"

The man might say or think:

- "There is so much going on at work. I have so much to do."

- "I wish I could just have some time to myself to relax and do something other than work."

The wife wants the relationship with the husband to fulfill her and the husband wants his work to fulfill him. Based on the woman's design, she has a basic need for security that is not being met. The man's basic need based on his design is significance and that is not being met.

The judgments set up relationships (and marriages in particular) to struggle and fail. But God has the answer!

REFLECTIVE QUESTIONS

- Think about your relationship with your spouse. List some ways you notice your *Flashing ME* impacting the relationship. Based upon meditating on scripture, speaking to a counselor, or changing your attitude, what do you need to do to change that?

  _____

  _____

  _____

- How does the issue of control impact your marriage and your family?

  _____

  _____

  _____

- Make a list of what you think needs to change based on the list in the prior question.

  _____

  _____

  _____

  _____

GOD'S SOLUTION

God can help marriages succeed and remove the judgments' impact. God's methods are always the best. He is the only one who can resolve the pain and struggles that come from the judgments that He established.

Real men and women follow God's direction so that relationships work. When a husband loves his wife like Christ loves the church, and a wife respects her husband as God asks, the judgments do not control their relationship.

A woman who *starts* respecting will *stop* controlling. A man who *starts* loving and pursuing his wife's best, will *stop* ruling her, abdicating leadership, and perform excellent work, because it is another way to glorify God. The power of God's ways easily handles the difficulties imposed by the judgments, unless either husband or wife start flashing their ME. When either of them flash their ME, the focus veers from ultimately glorifying God to serving self. God's formula works when husband and wife focus on pursuing their spouse's best.

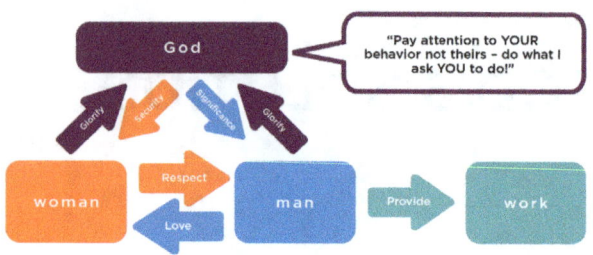

God says, "Pay attention to *your* behavior, not theirs. Do what I ask *you* to do!" That is the ONLY way that you will stop "flashing your ME"! The judgments get you to focus on how your needs are not being met and instead encourage a focus on getting other people or things to meet those needs. But—and this is important—God's statements are for each of us to choose, not for us to try to make others choose it. Yes, you are to speak God's truth into another person's life, but it is God's job to change them.

The power to overcome the judgments only comes from God. But (even though God can) He does not force us to choose His way. That is your responsibility.

He states that a wife is to respect her own husband (Ephesians 5:22) and that a husband is to love his wife as Christ loves the church (Ephesians 5:25-31). Please notice what God *does not* say. "Husbands get your wife to respect you. And, wives, make sure that your husband loves you."

Think about the statement above and how it might impact you interacting with your spouse! It might be eye-opening to see how that belief could impact your relationship with your husband or wife.

When you start focusing on what God asks of you, you stop participating in your judgment. The judgment focuses your attention on what the other person is doing or not doing. Start paying attention and changing your own behavior instead of looking for someone else to change, unless of course you enjoy and prefer the pain of the judgments.

Summary

To summarize, the very things that drive men and women are correlated to the judgments against them. Women may wonder why their need to relate seems to get sabotaged by their own actions. Men may struggle with their need to provide, protect, and preserve when that causes them to operate in their judgment, and drives their need to control the work.

Woman

- **Designed to RELATE:** The woman's design helps, nurtures, and supports relationships, especially with her husband and children.

- **RELATING is Judged:** The woman's judgment adds pain to relationships and drives her to control them, which creates more pain, especially with her husband and children.

Man

- **Designed to WORK:** The man's design provides, protects, and preserves others, especially his wife and children.
- **WORK is Judged:** The man's judgment adds pain to work and drives him to control work, which creates more pain, especially for his wife and children.

REFLECTIVE QUESTIONS

- How can you start respecting and not controlling your husband? What changes in your thinking will this require?

  _____

  _____

  _____

- Reflect on Ephesians 5:25-31.
  What does God say to you regarding how you show up in your marriage? What adjustments do you need to make?

  _____

  _____

  _____

- How is judgment impacting your relationship with your spouse or other important relationships? What can you do to live more by your God-given design?

  _____

  _____

  _____

  _____

STUDY GUIDE

Scripture Meditation

Time: 30 minutes a day

Each day read and meditate on one of the scriptures listed below or as directed by your session leader.
Follow these steps:

1. Get in a quiet place without distraction.
2. Play a praise song, and just listen to the words.
3. Ask God to reveal His heart and meaning to you as you read the scriptures.
4. Write your reflections below or in your journal.
5. Read the scriptures daily so you receive maximum revelation.

Genesis 3:16, NKJV	Titus 2:5, NKJV	Genesis 3:17-19, NKJV
Genesis 2:18, NKJV	Ephesians 5:25-31, NKJV	Genesis 4:7, NKJV
Titus 2:1-7, NKJV	1 Corinthians 11:3, NKJV	1 Timothy 2:14, NKJV

REFLECTIVE QUESTIONS

- When you get into conflicts with people over the next few months, stop and reflect on whether your ME is flashing. If you find it is, determine what you need to change.

_____

_____

_____

_____

_____

- A woman's unknown judgments include: Pain with Children, Desire for a Husband and Ruled by a Husband. How do you see this playing out in your relationship with your spouse? Do these judgments impact relationships beyond your marriage or a relationship with a significant other?

_____

_____

_____

_____

_____

- Adam's judgments include: He followed and did not lead, when Eve suggested he try the forbidden fruit. The second one was not a direct curse to Adam. The ground was cursed, which causes the third element, Adam's toil will be painful and he would be returned to dust. How do you see this conflicting with man's need and design to Preserve, Protect, and Provide?

_____

_____

_____

_____

- How does fear impact you and important relationships in your life? Reflect on what you can do to turn away from fear and embrace faith in God. (Possible ways fear plays out in your life are listed below.)
    - fear of needs not being met

_____

    - fear of losing control

_____

    - fear of failing

_____

- fear of not measuring up

_____

- fear of loneliness

_____

- fear of pain

_____

- fear of submitting

_____

- fear of not knowing

_____

- fear of serving others

_____

- How can you apply God's Solution of adhering
  to His design for you, to improve your
  relationships?

_____

_____

_____

_____

TOOLS

The following tools will enable you to understand yourself, your spouse, and how you can work together to handle conflict. The videos listed below are a part of the FREE video course that corresponds to the information in this book. Completing all the courses will be instrumental for you to find FREEDOM!

You can find all these tools (and many more) on our website www.GR8relate.com at the TOOLS tab.

Kolbe Assessment https://gr8relate.com/kolbe

You can trust the validity and accuracy of the Kolbe instrument to show you your strengths and instincts. The Kolbe also helps you easily see and understand how the strengths and talents of one person may not be considered as strengths by another. This critical information will help you bridge the gap between reality and your expectations of them. Once you complete the assessment, you will receive detailed reports that will help you understand your strengths and talents and how to use your strengths in a complementary way with your spouse, family member, or friend's strengths. By understanding your instincts you can more easily discuss your differences, laugh about them, and develop ways to deal with them.

The *Thomas-Kilman Conflict Mode Instrument* (TKI)   https://gr8relate.com/tki

The TKI is the world's best-selling instrument for understanding conflict. It helps you see that conflict can be beneficial and useful, instead of thinking conflict as bad. You will be provided detailed information on effectively using all five conflict modes: competing, collaborating, compromising, avoiding, and accommodating.

The *Fundamental Interpersonal Relations Orientation-Behavior* ™ (FIRO-B®). https://gr8relate.com/firob

The FIRO-B helps you understand how you interact at work and personal life. This easy-to-complete-assessment will provide critical insights into how an individual interacts with others. This personality instrument measures how you typically behave with others and how you expect them to act toward you.

Individual Videos

We have a FREE video course that corresponds with the information in this book.

These are short courses that you can watch/listen at your own pace. Enter the information in parenthesis below into your browser and you will be taken to a video course. When you are online, scroll down and click the "Sign Up / Start Course" button to create an account, or if you have one, sign up for the course. Yes, the courses are Free, the "sign up" will help you keep up with the courses you have completed.

There are two options:
- BOOK SERIES Courses: These are specific videos selected from the COMPLETE courses that help explain the contents of this book.
  - What Damages Relationships (https://gr8relate.com/video-courses/what-damages-relationships/)
- COMPLETE Courses: These are the original, complete courses that give you more details about the information in the book.
  - 04A - The Unknown Judgment for Women (https://gr8relate.com/video-courses/unknown-judgment-for-women/)

- 04B - The Unknown Judgment for Men (https://gr8relate.com/video-courses/unknown-judgment-for-men/)
- 04C – Battle Between Designs and Judgments (https://gr8relate.com/video-courses/battle-between-designs-and-judgments/)

TWO CIRCLES

1. _____ / _____
2. _____
3. _____

1. _____ / _____
2. _____
3. _____

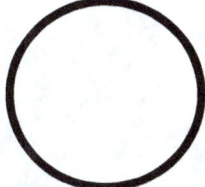

The PROBLEM and 4 Mistakes

The PROBLEM – Make Everything about ME

- Take everything personally by making your "ME" flash
- Live only by appetites, impulses, and pleasures
- Don't think— react/respond to everything emotionally
- Be happy, satisfied, and content only if people and circumstances are treating you right
- Only consider others when there is something in it for YOU.

> **James 3:16** – Where envy and self-seeking exist, confusion and every evil thing are there.
> **Philippians 2:3** – Let nothing be done through selfish ambition or conceit, but in lowliness of mind let each esteem others better than himself.

Operate on Opinion and Emotions – **The POLITICIAN**

- When we can't find or don't know the facts – we tend to "fill in the blanks"
- Opinion = judgment or belief not founded on certainty or proof; seem to be true or probable
- Emotions are RESPONDERS and often UNTRUSTWORTHY
- Objectivity = How it IS
- Subjectivity = How it FEELS
- "Who is my "who-said-so"?

> **Judges 21:25** – In those days there was no king in Israel; everyone did what was right in his own eyes.
> **Proverbs 3:5-6** – Trust in the LORD with all your heart, and lean not on your own understanding; in all your ways acknowledge Him, and He shall direct your paths

Keep the Past in the Present – **The VICTIM**

- Do not understand the power of forgiveness
- Do not understand the power of confession
- Do not understand that the PAST IS OVER
- Do not understand you are being controlled
- Good relationships leave a trail of resolved issues

> **Luke 17:3** – And if he sins against you seven times in a day, and seven times in a day returns to you, saying, 'I repent,' you shall forgive him.
> **1 John 1:9** – If we confess our sins, He is faithful and just to forgive us our sins and to cleanse us from all unrighteousness.

Wear a Mask – **The ACTOR**

- Acting or pretending, not being a REAL person
- "Walking on eggshells," dance around problems
- Not willing to seek or share the truth
- IMPLIES – I'm free to lie, but not free to tell the truth
- It takes 2 REAL people to have a REAL relationship

> **Ephesians 4:15** – ...but, speaking the truth in love, may grow up in all things into Him who is the head—Christ

Try to Change Others – **The DICTATOR**

- You think others should never be free to choose their path because they will mess things up
- You believe that other people must change to be like you want them
- You assign them a "JOB" to make you happy
- Reality is that the heart of a relationship is to know others for who they are and still accept, value, and love them.

> **Galatians 5:1** – Stand fast therefore in the liberty by which Christ has made us free, and do not be entangled again with a yoke of bondage.
> **Galatians 5:13** – For you, brethren, have been called to liberty; only do not use liberty as an opportunity for the flesh, but through love serve one another.

Personal Plan Form

1. THERE—Goals, Desired Outcomes (Picturable, Measurable, Specific)	Date	

Benefits for me:	Supports my values of:	

2. HERE—Current Reality	•	
•	•	
•	•	
•	•	
•	•	
•	•	
•	•	
•	•	

3. PATH—Actions	Progress Measures	Partners	Date
	Date Prepared		

This form is available as a Microsoft Word document for completion on a computer

Learn From The Past to Plan For The Future

Question 1: What were your greatest accomplishments in the last 12 months? Even if the last 12 months were the worst of your life, odds are, if you look hard enough, there's something somewhere to be proud of. If it was great, that makes answering the question even easier. After you've listed all your accomplishments, think about each one in detail. Identify several takeaways for each - what you learned or were reminded of by it.

Question 2: What were your biggest disappointments in the last 12 months? Practically every company and individual resists analyzing their mistakes. That's a shame because this is where great learning can happen. No matter how well everything is going, everyone makes mistakes. The trick here is to examine what preceded them, what you could have done differently, and how you can prevent making the same mistakes in the future. Even though the last 12 months were great, you will likely have some disappointments, both personally and professionally. As you did with your accomplishments, list your biggest disappointments - and then identify several takeaways for each one.

Question 3: How did you limit yourself in the past 12 months, and how can you remove those limits in the next 12 months? Were there certain actions you took or didn't take that came back to haunt you? Bring these actions to the surface, shine a light on them, and, most importantly, determine what you want to do differently now and in the future. Once again, make a list and identify the takeaways. For example, when I don't review my goals daily, I react and respond, getting pulled into what's currently happening and distracted from what may be more important. That reduces my actions on my goals. The takeaway: Commit to using the Daily Focus Form, and schedule key actions on my current day calendar to remind me.

Question 4: What did you learn from your answers to the first three questions? This is where you can get the best benefit from this exercise. Remember, the purpose of the exercise is not simply to know you and your business better, but actually use what you learn to help the next 12 months. What are your main takeaways from the first three questions? What do you now know about yourself or your business that you didn't realize or weren't thinking about before? Here are two items from my list...

- Creating products, coaching, and teaching are my biggest accomplishments. Therefore, it's easy to spend time daily creating materials and clarifying how to improve the material.
- A limiting factor is not focusing on attracting and acquiring more people to the material that I love to create. Marketing is inadequate, often ignored, and difficult for me.

Get as many takeaways as possible, because that is how you put your learning into reality. These takeaways can help make the next 12 months great. Of course, it's not enough to just make your list (although that, by itself, will get you part way there). You still need to take this information and USE IT! And that's where our final question comes in...

Question 5: How can you use this information to make the next 12 months great? The idea is to take everything that surfaced in your answers to the first 4 questions and build it into your schedule, your interactions, your management style, and so on. This may alter your goals or help you achieve them. Whatever you do, make sure you create goals first. For example, after I created my goals, I also added some specific actions to help me accomplish them.

- Started each morning with my Daily Focus Form.
- Block out marketing time on my weekly calendar
- Connect to some good marketing resources

S.M.A.R.T. Goals

S—SPECIFIC: The devil is in the specific details

- Clear, specific, and picturable
- Exactly what you want in concrete terms
- You will know your objective is specific enough if:
  - everyone involved knows the specifics of their involvement
  - everyone involved understands and is clear about the desired end result
  - your objective is free from jargon
  - you've defined all your terms
  - you've used only appropriate language
- These are not clear objectives
  - Increase quality time with my wife
  - Improve my writing skills
  - Create a more positive home environment
  - Regularly follow up with team members and direct reports
- These are good objectives
  - Spend at least 15 minutes each weekday morning with my wife
  - My small group rates my next three articles at 3.5 or better (1 to 5 scale)
  - Spend 30 to 60 minutes with each child each week
  - Meet for 15 minutes each workday morning to discuss yesterday's and today's top 3 tasks

S	• Specific: clear, picturable, free of jargon
M	• Measurable: you and others can know it was done (quantity, dollars, time, quality...)
A	• Acceptable : within your control / influence, practical, realistic
R	• Result-Oriented: serves the organization's purpose and objectives, results not actions
T	• Time-bound: clear target date, deadline for completion

M—MEASURABLE: Critical Element

- You will know you've achieved your objective because the metric is the evidence. Others can know too! It becomes your statement of success.
- Objectives must have some method of tracking progress, measuring success over time
- Current Reality (HERE) is imperative for metrics
  - How would you measure weight loss if you did not know how much you weighed?
  - How do you measure employee retention if you do not know the current turnover?
  - Establish baselines (current reality) and measure progress from that point
- Objectives are not masters; they are servants supporting personal / company values and purpose
- Define the deliverables, documents, products, and accomplishments desired

HERE (Current Reality) Checklist

Did you use your Future Result as a reference point in describing current reality?

End Result	Current Reality
100% on-time delivery	89% on-time delivery in last 3 months
$48 million in annual sales	$31 million in sales in past fiscal year

Have you described the relevant picture? It must be relevant to the Future Result. No unrelated details.

End Result	Irrelevant Details
100% on-time delivery	Product packaged in blue box
$48 million in annual sales	Sales tax is captured at point of sale

Have you included the whole picture? It is not enough to say "I don't have (my future result)".

Rather Than	Write
We don't have a quality program	We don't have a formal system although people see a need for more quality in our products. Customer surveys report dissatisfaction with our current quality. We have a training specialist in-house that has had some experience with quality, and the management team is overworked and a bit resistant to any change right now.

Translate assumptions and editorials into objective news reports. We just want facts. Objective current reality allows the design of effective actions to help create the results we want.

Editorial	Facts
We don't have any business trying to go after business outside our niche market	We have tried to do business outside of our market, but we got only a small return on our investment. We didn't know how to do it.

Have you told the story without exaggeration? Better or worse than reality is not helpful.

Exaggeration	Current Reality
Our products are rated the best	One of three product surveys rated us #1. The other two rated us #4.
We have the worst record on safety	We had 9 near misses and 1 minor accident this past year

Did you state what reality is or how it got that way? Just describe "right now", not the past.

"The Journey"	Current Reality
We bought a new kettle for the plant, and by the time we installed it, the sales guys had drummed up so many new orders that we couldn't keep up. So we had to put on a new shift, but they were untrained and we didn't make a lot of headway, but our costs went up. The customers weren't getting their orders when we promised, and everyone was mad at us and blaming us, but it was really the fault of the sales guys over promising again.	Capacity is strained, more orders than we can handle. Sales and manufacturing are not coordinated. New people have taken more time than we thought to come up to speed. Costs up from adding new shift.

Have you included all the facts you need? Leaving an element out of current reality is the same as not giving the whole story.

Current sales	Current management strategies and attitudes
Current market trends	Current job market and hiring practices
Current market share	Current systems
Current competition	Current talent of members of the organization
Current financial conditions	Current core competencies
Current product quality	Current decision-making process
Current distribution system	Current business approach
Current capacity	Available resources
What you need	What you do not know
What could help	What could hurt

Pursuing their BEST
– in Work, in Life, in Love

Daily Focus Form

Date: ___/___/___

Directions

1. Do MY PROJECTS and MY CONTACTS before you do MY TODAY
2. Schedule three 60-minute slots today for items below
3. Write and review items for 7 and 30 days for your projects
4. Write all intends or ideas on the other side of this sheet
5. 1-week rule – Delete, Do, Schedule, or list on back

Time Principles

1. Limited Resource
2. Inflexible Resource
3. Always More Things to Do Than Time Available
4. *Focus (Not Efficiency) is the Key to Mastering Time*

MY FOCUS FOR TODAY (No more than 3!)

Top 3	Next 3-5

MY CONTACTS

People I need to contact today to help me accomplish my goals and projects

Could Help My Goals / Projects	Follow Up or Waiting on Them
•	•
•	•
•	•
•	•

MY PROJECTS

3-5 things I need to do in the next 7 and 30 DAYS to move each project forward

Next 7 Days	Next 30 Days
PROJECT 1 –	
PROJECT 2 –	
PROJECT 3 –	
PROJECT 4 –	

242 Spring Park Drive, Ste A   Midland, Texas 79705   Phone: 432-682-6823   https://gr8relate.com   Email: info.gr8relate@gr8grp.com

Focus Triangle

COMMIT

ATTEMPT

INTEND

242 Spring Park Drive, Ste A   Midland, Texas 79705   Phone: 432-682-6823   https://gr8relate.com   Email: support@gr8relate.com

ENDNOTES

1   Henry, M. (1994). Matthew Henry's commentary
    on the whole Bible: complete and unabridged in one
    volume (p. 14). Hendrickson.